*Dedicated to my three greatest blessings*
*Bohemia, Riva & Laveau*

# INTRODUCTION

Welcome to the book that could totally change your life. I know that's a big hype up for my first ever self-published book, but it could just be true.

I was introduced to the idea of 21, 28 or 30 day gratitude practices over fifteen years ago and they have Changed. My. Life! **I really want this to change yours too.**

Firstly, thank you for choosing this book and trusting me to direct your energy and efforts in the right place. Simply by changing your thoughts consciously for the next 22 days you have the ability to totally change your life. hope that you are as excited for this process as I am because that excitement and anticipation really is a vital factor for this to work. You HAVE to be excited that this is the key, this is the answer, this is going to shift something in you, this is going to dissolve an energy that's been stuck and dragging you down.

The great thing is, that excitement for the process is a self fulfilling prophecy. The first time you do this book you're excited and that creates a vibrational shift in itself. You have a great result at the end of the 22 days and so the next time you do it, even before you've picked up the book your vibration is raised by the prospect of having a similar result. The book itself takes on its own vibration and holds a space for you to manifest miracles.

In the past these gratitude practices were well-known in my circle of friends and family for changing my life. Like, dramatically. One time I did it and finally decided to walk away from a marriage that made me so sad, another time I got pregnant with my twin daughters & another time saw the resolution of a personal life problem that had plagued me and almost destroyed me for over a year of my life. Each time this simple practice of cultivating gratitude in various ways over the period of a month transformed me. Solutions came from places I never expected. People, situations and opportunities seemed to manifest out of thin air. My mindset changed everything, both internally and externally too.

I look back at all the times I had reached rock bottom and turned to a gratitude practice to change something - anything! What was the secret sauce?

**1. You have to be excited.**

**2. You have to be open to whatever might happen.**

**3. You have to believe in the power of your thoughts to change your life.**

**4. You HAVE to stick to it! If you skip a day or forget about it for a weekend, it won't work.**

So all I ask is that you give me your time, energy and focus for the next 21 days, that we do this together & that you're totally open to the miracles that may unfold for you.

If you find it hard doing this alone find a buddy to keep you accountable. I never, ever managed to finish these kinds of things until I did it alongside my two best friends and that's when the *magic* happened.

Embarking on a journey towards your goals can often feel like a solitary venture, but the power of a like-minded community can transform your journey into an exciting adventure. Research indicates that the mere act of sharing your aspirations with others significantly enhances your chances of success—people are 65% more likely to achieve their goals when they commit to someone else. This collaborative spirit not only provides a robust support system but also injects an infectious motivation that propels individuals to new heights. Picture this: you're part of a group of individuals who share your vision, encouraging each other with unwavering support during challenges.

Studies show that those who engage in group-based interventions are more successful in achieving and sustaining their objectives, creating a positive atmosphere of shared triumphs and camaraderie. This positive peer pressure becomes a driving force, fostering healthy competition and propelling everyone toward excellence. Moreover, the exchange of knowledge within such a community becomes a treasure trove of insights, accelerating your progress through shared experiences and collective wisdom. So, surround yourself with those who resonate with your goals, as the journey becomes not just yours but a collective voyage towards success. This is all well and good but what if you don't have likeminded people in your life?

Well I didn't either massively.

If you don't have someone who's as up for it as you are, you can do it with me in my self development book club! Simply join via *francescaamber.com* and listen to a new podcast episode each morning for 21 days. We also have a Facebook support group where we share our insights and progress. You would be amazed at what a difference it makes doing it with likeminded people. The book club bitches have been an amazing accountability and support over the years and I would love you to join us!

One last thing I'd say before we start is to be aware of the timing of your life. If you have lots of nights out or a holiday or something planned over the next few weeks, now might not be the ideal time to do this. Although we SHOULD make time and space for gratitude every day, the reality is - this is going to take up some of your energy and you need to really show up for it. I personally like to do this on the 1st of every January to start the year off with a bang but you can begin this 21 day practice whenever you like.

**Ok are we ready?  Let's go!**

# DAY ONE
*The Power of Gratitude*

If you are new to practicing gratitude, or like me you often forget about it in the busyness of life, a morning gratitude list is the simplest & most transformative place to start.

Due to an ancient thought bias designed to keep us safe, our brains will (annoyingly) focus on the negatives in our lives. This is because negative people, comments and experiences are most likely to cause us harm, and so our delightful lizard brains harp on it, repeating it over and over in our minds like some sick horror movie.

The problem is this distorts the reality of that small, minor negative experience. You might have experienced this when posting a picture on social media and getting lots of lovely comments from your friends and family. You quickly focus in one the one comment from some anonymous troll (probably your ex sitting in his y-fronts) saying you look like shit. You tend to hyper focus on that one negative comment because that's the one that (if it were true) could affect your happiness and safety.

Unfortunately, our brains don't shine a similar spotlight on all of the positive comments, people and experiences in our lives. That's why we must cultivate a habit of looking for the good in everything and showing gratitude for all the positive aspects of our lives that are happening every day. Remember, what you focus on, grows. So as you start to recognise and celebrate the good things, they will continue to show up in bigger and better ways in your life.

We are going to start today and every day for the rest of this book with a morning gratitude list. Doing this one practice alone has absolutely transformative effects. The reason we do it first thing in the morning, is because it's going to set the tone for our entire day. Also, we can quickly get distracted by the pulls of life, whether that's a screaming child that wants ice cream for breakfast or a long commute that's been made even longer by a closed road. Do it first thing, before you even get out of bed and it is done and dusted before you've had your morning shower.

In the past I've completed different gratitude practices that have asked you to list 10 things to be thankful about every morning, but I find that to be a little excessive and so we are going to start with a list of 20 blessings today then going forward, three blessings that relate to your day.

If you are struggling to come up with twenty blessings in your life, I'll give you a virtual slap round the face right now. Think about your life, do you have a bed to sleep in, a home to wake up in? Family and friends? A job? Money in your bank account? Your health, can you get up and walk, move your arms and take yourself to the toilet?

Can you see and hear? Is your day today going to depend on war or are you living in a peaceful country? Do you have food to eat and water to drink today? There are SO many things to be thankful for when you look around. In the words of Phil Collins - 'it's just another day for you and me in paradise.'

**Write your list of blessings in the following format:**

*I am so thankful for ......... because ......... so thank you, thank you, THANK YOU universe!*

We amplify our gratitude when we think about WHY we're thankful and say thank you three times. Three is the number of creation and truly, you can't say thank you enough.

For example: I am so thankful I have a house, somewhere to call home, because it is the backdrop to the movie of my life. It is somewhere to rest my head at night, binge Netflix on the cold winter nights, have BBQs with my friends in the summer, raise my children, take care of myself and live out our lives in comfort. Thank you, thank you, THANK YOU universe!

Once you have completed the list read all twenty back to yourself (out loud, if you can).

Now, today was an upside-down-over-a-beer-keg-style blast in the face of gratitude but the following mornings your gratitude list will be like a little after breakfast limoncello shot. I want you to write just THREE blessings you're truly thankful for that relate to that specific day.

**For example:**

I'm so thankful my favourite band decided to on tour and I get to see them perform live tonight because not many people get this opportunity. Thank you, thank you, THANK YOU universe!

*Or*

I'm so thankful I have a lunch date booked in with my best friend today because I want to hear all about her latest dick appointment and she really raises my vibe. Thank you, thank you, THANK YOU universe!

Keep a notebook and pen beside your bed so you don't forget (or have to go hunting for a pen first thing in the morning) and commit to this simple practice for the next 21 days. It takes mere minutes yet the effects cumulatively will astound you.

## Day One Exercise:

Write a gratitude list of **TWENTY** blessings in your life and don't forget to say thank you, thank you, THANK YOU universe for each one.

**Share your progress with me.**

Tag me on Instagram! I'm **@francecsaamber**

Use the hashtag **#gratefulAFbook**

# DAY TWO

*Manifest Whilst You Sleep*

Yesterday we focussed on starting our day with gratitude and today we're going to close our day with gratitude too. Why? Well, science has shown that our brains go into a theta brainwave state, similar to hypnosis as we fall asleep and as we wake up.

This hypnotic phase, known as the theta state, is a bridge between wakefulness and the depths of sleep. As our surroundings grow dim and our thoughts start to meander, our brain's electrical activity slows, and the dominant frequency shifts to the gentle rhythm of theta waves, typically ranging from 4 to 7 Hz. In this state, our mind becomes highly receptive to suggestions and creative inspiration, making it a ripe setting for self-reflection, setting intentions, vivid dreams, and even therapeutic hypnosis.

It's during these moments of theta-wave dominance that the mysterious landscapes of our subconscious mind unfold, carrying us into the powerful realm of sleep, where subconscious work and renewal await.

A major part of my positive bedtime routine is to get into the habit of regularly listening to subliminals. I've been listening to subliminals for the past two years and it's had a dramatic effect on my life. Not only are they powerful, but so easy to insert into my daily rituals. As a busy mum of three, some days I don't work on my mindset or goals at all apart from listening to subliminals whilst I relax or sleep.

So what is a subliminal? Well, subliminal messaging operates on the subtle, almost imperceptible border between conscious awareness and the subconscious mind. It involves conveying messages or stimuli that are intentionally concealed from our conscious perception, typically through brief flashes, low-volume sounds, or hidden imagery. These concealed messages bypass our conscious scrutiny but still register in our subconscious, influencing our thoughts, feelings, and behaviours.

The theory behind subliminal messaging suggests that these hidden cues can shape our attitudes or prompt us to take specific actions without our conscious awareness. Dangerous when huge junk food companies are using them without our knowledge, but powerful when we intentionally listen to them on our terms to manifest positive aspects into our lives.

I have created a number of subliminals ranging from wealth, health, fertility, happiness, beauty, confidence & more. But I would like to gift you the 'gratitude' version to listen to each night during this process. Simply download to your phone and access in your 'files' to listen even when you're on airplane mode. Listen with the volume at a comfortable level (for me this is quite low whilst I'm sleeping) and don't worry that you don't hear any affirmations. Beneath the relaxing music (which is set to the healing frequency no less, you're welcome) there are hundreds of positive affirmations about gratitude and abundance beneath the music. Drift off knowing that you are literally manifesting in your sleep!

Play nightly or during any quiet time in the day (cooking, crafting or bath time) for at least 30 days and see the difference.

Sign up to my mailing list on *francescaamber.com* to receive a free subliminal in your inbox. This is the gratitude subliminal you need to listen to every night for the rest of this process.

## Day Two Exercise:

List three blessings you are grateful for as you wake up or as early in the day as you can. Make them specific to your day for bonus gratitude points!

Download my free subliminal and listen each night as you go to sleep (or in the daytime if during sleep really isn't possible) for at least 30 days.

**Share your progress with me.**

Tag me on Instagram! I'm **@francecsaamber**

Use the hashtag **#gratefulAFbook**

# DAY THREE

*Gratitude For Family*

When we start to think about our blessings and what we're thankful for, our minds very often head straight to our friends and family. Rightly so! Our lives are enriched massively by the people in our lives and our families usually top the list. We may not get to choose our family but they often are the people who are there for us no matter what, through thick and thin. Today we're going to focus our gratitude practice on the family in our lives.

Now, if you have a tumultuous relationship with your family or perhaps don't even know your family at all - this practice is still for you. The universe wants us to learn that gratitude, true gratitude is being thankful for EXACTLY what you have, no matter how little or much you have. Imagine if I wasn't grateful for my job as a podcaster because it wasn't as big or successful as the Parenting Hell podcast? Or I wasn't thankful for my health because I'm not an olympic swimmer, I can only swim 20 meters? It makes ZERO sense. So, today I want you to be thankful for your family no matter what the quality of that is in your life.

If you were to be negative you could look at this exercise

and say 'but I don't get along with my dad and he has been the source of so many struggles for me' but that isn't showing gratitude for the dad that you have. Instead you could say a number of reasons to be grateful:

'I'm so thankful my dad left so that our family could recover in peace.'
'I'm so thankful my dad has shown me what I don't want to be in my own life.'
'I'm so thankful my dad has made me enforce boundaries so that nobody else can take advantage of me.'

We are training our brain to find the good in every aspect of our lives, even if it feels lacking to us.

I want you to pick three people in your family to focus your gratitude on. Pick three people you are closest to or have the most gratitude for.

Today you are going to write them a letter, email or text, detailing everything you're thankful for about them. If it helps, you can write it in a list format, as we do with our morning gratitude list. For example:

Mum, I'm so thankful you are always there to support me when I need you. Thank you, thank you, THANK YOU!

Dad, I'm so thankful you have alternative views and opinions that have helped me have a more open mind. Thank you, thank you, THANK YOU!

This exercise today is truly a gift for both you and the recipient. To feel gratitude is one thing, but to express that gratitude has a huge effect on both people. Some of us will have never had the courage to say what we really want to say, and doing it in the format of 'I'm reading this book and it gave me this exercise to do...' is an easy way of being open about your feelings.

Don't underestimate the effects of your words on the recipient. Know that by giving them this gift today you are bringing someone so much joy.

Don't overthink the process or delay until another day - write and deliver all three lists or letters today.

As you list all the things you love about that person and hit send you will be overcome with love and gratitude which will boost your vibration sky high.

## Day Three Exercise:

List three things each morning (or as early in the day as you can) that you're thankful for. Bonus gratitude points if you can make them relevant to your day.

Take three members of your family and write a gratitude list for each one. You can turn the list into a letter or just keep it as a list but SHARE it with each person, telling them how thankful you are that they are in your life.

Listen to your gratitude subliminal as you go to sleep tonight.

**Share your progress with me.**

Tag me on Instagram! I'm **@francecsaamber**

Use the hashtag **#gratefulAFbook**

# DAY FOUR

*There's No Place Like Home*

Your home is the backdrop to the movie of your life and the foundation for so many elements of your life to rest upon. Some of us will be more affected by our home environment than others, but there is no doubt that your environment and how you live is having a direct impact on the quality of your life.

Something that greatly interests me is the concept of 'spacial alchemy'. This is a term coined by Olga Naiman, an interior designer who understands that how you create your home is going to have a huge impact on how you live your life.

How we design our home and the rooms within it will affect how we use them and how we use them will determine how we live and how we live will impact the life we are able to create.

For example, if your kitchen is cluttered and dirty, you have no storage and nowhere to sit and eat it's unlikely that you have healthy eating habits.

If you have an old bed with a tonne of clutter under it and broken curtains you are unlikely to get good quality sleep.

If you have an overstuffed wardrobe with overflowing drawers and no organisation it's unlikely that you're dressing for the life that you want.

If your office is chaos, littered with boxes and piles of stuff with a desk filled with papers, books and old mugs with mouldy tea in it's unlikely you're feeling productive and inspired when you go to work.

On a slightly bigger scale - if our homes are cluttered, messy and uninviting we are unlikely to want to share them with our friends, family or potential new partners which is robbing us of so many fun times and happy memories.

As you can see, how our rooms are organised and kept has a big impact on what they offer us in life. They can either hinder us or be the biggest aide in achieving our goals. This is why it's imperative we design our homes to help us succeed, whether the goal is to eat better, workout, start a business or dress beautifully every day.

As a successful habits expert who I can't remember once said: 'the most successful people are those who don't have to use their willpower to overcome their surroundings'.

Our homes should be a source of peace and joy, a sanctuary from the outside world, a place to enjoy, connect, rest and restore. Think about your home now. Is it a source or stress? Or is it a source of joy?

Is your home an obstacle to overcome before you get to

work on your goals and live your best life or is it set up to help you?

I could write an entire book on what our homes should be to us (and I think I will!) But for now I want you to take part in this beautiful practice with your home.

We are going to physically and energetically clean and clear our front door/porch/entrance to our home. In Feng shui the entrance to the home is very important as this is where all the energy enters your home. Cleaning, clearing and decorating it is highly symbolic and will bring you nothing but good fortune and high vibes.

If you live in a flat you can still do this with your internal door and if you live with others I'm sure they will be very thankful for you creating this gorgeous entrance to your home.

First of all, clear away any clutter or obstructions from the front door area, both sides of the door. We want the area to be clear to welcome in opportunities and abundance. Next we clean. Sweep the steps and get rid of the cobwebs. Take some warm water and a beautiful smelling cleaner and clean down your front door. You can go full on with this if you wish and add a new mat or hang a flower wreath to say thank you to your home.

The important part is that we carry out this task with intention. This isn't just cleaning your front door for the sake of it, the benefit is twofold.

Firstly, we are telling the universe with our physical actions (the universe bloody loves an action) that we are serious about welcoming in good energy to our homes and lives and secondly, we are showing gratitude to our home (no matter how much you love it currently) for taking care of us and our possessions. As you clean you can say in your head or out loud how thankful you are to your home.

I try to do this practice about once a season, change up my wreath or plants to wake up the energy. By the way faux flower wreaths aren't great Feng shui but I LOVE them, so I think the joy of seeing my beautiful wreath every day outweighs any negatives.

I also have an evil eye I bought in Morocco hanging so that it wards off any negative people that may darken my doorstep. Do what feels right for you and have fun with it! You can get incredible handmade door knockers these days, paint your front door an amazing colour (thank the lord for UPVC paint) hang seasonal wreaths, plant beautiful flowers either side of your door, get a welcome mat that shows your personality, change the outside light to one you love, the list is endless!

This practice takes less than an hour but the gratitude you should feel for your home should be increased by the end of it AND you end up with a gorgeous new entrance to your home to greet you every day.

It's the little things like this that add up and make a big difference to your daily gratitude. I wish I could share some of my Ring doorbell footage that shows the embarrassingly high number of times I get out my car and just ADMIRE my front porch. It could be raining, I've got 100 bags to carry in or a child is crying but I can't help but stop and admire my shiny black door, seasonal wreath, spiral topiary bookending each side of the steps and a hanging evil eye sparkling in the sun. It brings me JOY on my darkest days and I want you to experience that too.

On the flip side, I have a flat in London that I've had since my mid twenties and it is in a bit of a grotty building. The front door is directly onto a big road so is ALWAYS filthy and the communal entrance/stairs is grotty to say the least. Whenever I turn up there I feel a bit disappointed and rush to get inside my apartment. That ain't the vibe and always puts a slight dampener on what was otherwise a big goal of mine - to have a house in the country and a pied-a-terre in the city.

So basically, your door and your entrance matter!

Many practice Shinto beliefs including our favourite decluttering expert Marie Kondo. People with Shinto beliefs say that their home and their possessions have a soul and a vibration and will treat them accordingly. It's far too much to go into here but check it out if it interests you. I certainly believe my homes have souls and each time I leave my home I say (out loud, ha ha) thank you house for keeping everything safe and dry for me whilst I'm out. I often tell my home I love it too. Let me live my life!

## Day Four Exercise:

List three things you are grateful for as you wake up or as early in the day as you can. Make them specific to your day for bonus gratitude points!

Physically and energetically declutter and clean the entrance to your home.

Download my free subliminal and listen each night as you go to sleep (or in the daytime if during sleep really isn't possible) for at least 30 days.

**Share your progress with me.**

Tag me on Instagram! I'm **@francecsaamber**

Use the hashtag **#gratefulAFbook**

# DAY FIVE

*Peaks and Pits*

Today's gratitude exercise can be done in solitude or as part of a beautiful dinner or bedtime ritual. Perhaps like me you might want to do it with your partner or children as part of THEIR bedtime routine. I find the routine of kid's bedtimes are so much better than my own (I mean, how many times do they binge watch murder documentaries until 1am or fall into bed fully clothed after a bottle of rose with friends? Exactly!) The other benefit of course is that THEY start to get into the habit of practicing gratitude which fosters a great daily connection and of course will benefit the whole household.

If you work shifts or nights or bedtimes are just erratic for you then feel free to do this at a time that is consistent every day such as your evening meal or bath time (The Kardashians like to do it over dinner and I'm down for whatever the Kris Jenner does tbh!)

As you unwind for sleep or sit down to eat, replay your day through your mind and find what your FAVOURITE moment in the day was. Was it as you woke up and the sun was streaming through onto your bed? Was it chatting with a good friend after work? Was it realising a brand new episode of Keeping Up With The Kardashians had just dropped (Yessss!) Or getting a huge cuddle from your child after school? As you sort through your memories of the day, your brain is focussing on all the GOOD things that happened (see what we're doing here?) Find the very best one and say 'thank you universe' for that moment.

For the purposes of this book we're only focussing on the gratitude right now, but if this does become a new part of your dinner/bath/bedtime routine with your partner or children, try introducing an additional question: 'What was the hardest/worst thing that happened today?' I've found this fosters a great habit of being open with struggles or worries.

The amount of times I have asked my daughter how her day was to which she replies 'fine' only to reveal during our bedtime reflection on the day that a friend had refused to play with her or she was worried about something.

Ensure you finish with the 'favourite thing that happened today' question to end on a high, but including the 'worst thing that happened today' avoids toxic positivity and allows your partner or child (or who knows, flat mate, AirBNB guest, Tinder date?!) to be open with you.

## Day Five Exercise:

List three things you are grateful for as you wake up or as early in the day as you can. Make them specific to your day for bonus gratitude points!

During the most consistent part of your evening routine, whether that's dinner, bath or bed time, think about the best thing that happened to you that day. What was your favourite part?

If you live with others you could make this a daily bonding exercise.

Open up my free subliminal and listen each night as you go to sleep (or in the daytime if during sleep really isn't possible) for at least 30 days.

**Share your progress with me.**

Tag me on Instagram! I'm **@francecsaamber**

Use the hashtag **#gratefulAFbook**

# DAY SIX

*Gratitude for Friends*

On day three of this gratitude process we picked three members of our family and expressed our gratitude for them. Today is an even more powerful version of that because we are repeating the exercise for our friends.

The reason this is an even more powerful gratitude practice is because our family are bound to us by blood. You only need to become a mother to experience the strong biological urge to protect and nurture your child. But your friends don't have this. Your friends are in your life because they CHOSE to be. What a beautiful thing that is.

Today, I want you to choose three friends and think about why you are so thankful to have them in your life. You don't have to choose your three closest friends, just the ones you feel the most gratitude towards. You might choose a work colleague who gets you through the longest shifts or a childhood friend who has been there through all the ups and downs of life.

As you write each list, truly feel the gratitude and take a moment to imagine what life would be like without this person in your life. Once your list for each friend is complete it's time for the fun part! Share your list with your friend and imagine the surprise and joy when they open the email, message or letter (if you're feeling old school!)

As with the family, if you feel a little uncomfortable suddenly sharing so much gratitude - feel free to preface it with 'I'm currently reading this book which is all about gratitude and today's exercise was to show gratitude to my friends - so here's a list of all the things I'm thankful for about you.'

As you share your lists with your friends you should feel an overwhelming sense of gratitude for all the special relationships you have in your life. Bonus points for sharing your love on social media - who doesn't love a public shout out?

## Day Six Exercise:

List three things you are grateful for as you wake up or as early in the day as you can. Make them specific to your day for bonus gratitude points.

Pick three friends that you are so thankful for in your life. Write a list of everything you are thankful for in each one then share it with them.

Open my free subliminal and listen each night as you go to sleep (or in the daytime if during sleep really isn't possible) for at least 30 days.

**Share your progress with me.**

Tag me on Instagram! I'm **@francecsaamber**

Use the hashtag **#gratefulAFbook**

# DAY SEVEN
*Gratitude For Health*

One of the most obvious aspects of our lives to be grateful for is ironically the one thing we take for granted the most and that is our health.

We only need to experience slight inconveniences with our health to suddenly appreciate how important it is to us. A sudden tooth ache or a dodgy stomach before a big date? Nooooo! I will give anything, just give me my health back!

Many years ago I was good friends with a big Hollywood producer who I met in a club one night. Anyway, as our friendship progressed he invited me to fly out to Vegas with him to a party with JENNIFER LOPEZ! Can you imagine? I got myself a spray tan, a hot dress and boarded that flight ready to have the time of my life.

When we got to the gorgeous penthouse suite I ordered a steak with chips, sauce, probably green beans and a dessert on room service, ate the entire thing and began to get ready.

This is when 'the trouble' started. As I showered I had a sudden thought. 'I'm going to shit myself.' I prayed it was a one off but no. No, no, no. It becomes clear that I am at the beginning of a violent bout of diarrhoea. Was it brought on by the flight? The nerves? The prospect of having to share a room with a guy I didn't know that well? Or was it that goddamn steak? We'll never ever know but as I continued to gingerly get ready and ignore my symptoms I knew I wasn't going to make it. I got into the lift to go downstairs but as we walked across the lobby of the hotel I knew I couldn't go and had to return to the room alone.

He came back much later that night with tales of all the celebrities that were there, the free bar and amazing time he'd had. What had I been doing? Emptying my bowels every 30 minutes and watching ridiculously long drug commercials on the hotel TV.

Why am I sharing this rather embarrassing story with you? Because it shows that you can have the fancy date who flies you out to Vegas, the perfect spray tan, the cutest dress, the most amazing party to attend... but if you don't have your health it all means nothing. Jennifer Lopez could have been giving me a one woman show right there in the suite, but with the way my stomach was cramping and expelling everything I had ever consumed I would not have cared one bit.

Be thankful for your health, y'all!

Today I want you to think about every part of your body that you're thankful for and be thorough. Make a list in the same format as our morning gratitude lists:

I am so thankful for my brain as it enables me to create,

work and enjoy life. Thank you, thank you, THANK YOU universe!

I am so grateful for my eyesight as it means I can be independent, see where I'm going, take in the beautiful faces of my children and drive. Thank you, thank you, THANK YOU universe!

I am so thankful for my legs which help me to get around each day. I can walk, run, jump, drive, ride a bike, ride a horse, ride a camel, ride a man - there's no stopping me!

These are just a few examples of the MANY ways we can be thankful for our health. So write it out and feel that gratitude for your health like you never have before.

## Day Seven Exercise:

List three things you are grateful for as you wake up or as early in the day as you can. Make them specific to your day for bonus gratitude points!

Think about your health and write a gratitude list of every function and part of your body that is working for you. Today, take the time to reflect on how thankful you are for your health.

Open my free subliminal and listen each night as you go to sleep (or in the daytime if during sleep really isn't possible) for at least 30 days.

**Share your progress with me.**

Tag me on Instagram! I'm **@francecsaamber**

Use the hashtag **#gratefulAFbook**

# DAY EIGHT

*Gratitude for Wealth*

Congratulations! By now you have been showing gratitude for a full week? How do you feel? You should be feeling on a higher vibration and excited that as you continue to practice gratitude, your body and mind are actually changing at a biological level, as well as bring amazing things into your life.

Studies have shown that expressing gratitude can improve sleep, mood and immunity. Gratitude can also decrease depression, anxiety and difficulties with chronic pain. (Source, Mayo Clinic Health System) It also causes physiological changes in your body that initiate the parasympathetic nervous system - the part of your nervous system that helps you to rest and digest. (Source, UCLA Health)

Today we are going to focus our gratitude on wealth, no matter how much we have. Money and wealth can be such a tough topic lfor many reasons. Maybe you feel a lack of money in your life and it's hard to be thankful for the little you have. Perhaps you grew up with a negative money mindset and you perceive it as 'wrong' to celebrate money, appreciate material items or want more. This was me. There are still moments I feel 'icky' about the abundance I have or how I celebrate but you just have to keep working through your old money story and money blocks to keep welcoming new abundance in.

There are so many books that delve into money mindset work, how you can eliminate limiting beliefs and money blocks that are holding you back. You might be drawn to the more spiritual path of someone like Amanda Frances. Or you may find power in the more practical 'Rich Dad Poor Dad' approach. Either way, you are sure to find an author out there to resonate with you. I fell in love with the process of working on your money mindset so much that I created my own 3 week workshop all about manifesting money. (You can find it at francescaamber.com). Today we are simply focussing on showing and feeling gratitude for the money you have right now.

Think about all the money you have right now. If you have a job currently you are better off than the 2.5 million unemployed in this world. If you are reading this book in your home you are better off than the 1.5 million people worldwide who are homeless. If you ate enough today you are better off than the 3 billion people worldwide who can't afford to eat. Did you know that one in ten people go to bed hungry every night. One in TEN? Are you feeling more gratitude for your money already?

Think about all the money you have in your life right now outside of pounds in the bank. It could be in the form of equity in your house, a paid off car outside, a holiday already paid for, gift cards not yet used, clothes and toiletries ready to be used.

Think of all the things you buy with money. A home, electricity, fresh water, food, travel by car or train or bus, clothes to wear, toiletries to keep clean, detergent to wash your clothes, shampoo to wash your hair, fun nights out with your friends, your favourite books (of which I hope this is one!) A TV to watch on cold, dark evenings. Maybe even holidays? There are so many essential and more frivolous but fun things that our money pays for that enrich our lives beyond imagination.

Think about all the money you've been given in the past. Think about everything your parents or caregivers bought to bring you up. Think about the education you had, the birthday and Christmas presents you received, the trips and holidays you went on, the food you ate, the bedroom you slept in. As we get older we receive much less from our parents but we still continue to receive in so many other ways. Have you gone on dates where your date has paid for dinner? Have your friends treated you? Have boyfriends or girlfriends supported you financially? Maybe you had a questionable young adulthood like me and had a sugar daddy?

Even though we pay our taxes there were periods where as young adults in education or whilst we're out of work we didn't - and yet we still received street lighting and cleaning, road maintenance so we can get places, education, the right to see a doctor or go to hospital. Here in the UK we can have a baby and not get into debt for the pleasure of giving birth. We're SO lucky!

Today I want you to contact three people and thank them for bringing money into your life.

Your message could look like these:

*Mart, I'm so thankful you told me to move my podcast to Acast because before then I never had any sponsors of the show and monetising my hard work was... hard work! I now have a beautiful passive income stream so THANK YOU!*

*Mum, I'm so thankful as a single mum for all the clothes, food, experiences and comfortable home you provided me with as a child. Thank you so much.*

*Or*

*Yusuf, thank you so much for being my sugar daddy and sponsoring my goddamn life in my early twenties. You enabled me to leave home at a difficult time, find my feet and establish stability with my own flat in London and that was so important to me. You're welcome for my titillating dinner convo & the nudes. THANK YOU!*

If you feel compelled to do more than three, do! Keep the gratitude going! I can think of so many people who have brought money into my life it's insane!

My sister who loaned me money to buy my first house, my first boyfriend who bought me half a car for my birthday, Buzzsprout who taught me for free how to start a podcast, my friend who took me on a free cruise, an ex who would take me out to dinner and never let me pay, my listeners who have bought my products and supported the show... it goes on and on when you think about it.

As always, the gratitude is most powerful when we share it, so share away with those you are grateful for and feel your vibe rise and rise.

If you want some extra gratitude points, something I like to do to show gratitude to my money is get the highest denomination note you can afford, write 'THANK YOU' across it and frame it. I have a framed £50 note which I had hung in the hallway of my tiny old house and people must have thought I was crazy. But I had this vision that one day that same £50 note would be hung, pride of place above my front door in a grand hallway of my dream home. Spoiler alert - it is! Every day, each time I leave and enter my home, I walk under that sacred note and think 'thank you' for everything money has given me.

## Day Eight Exercise:

List three things you are grateful for as you wake up or as early in the day as you can. Make them specific to your day for bonus gratitude points!

Think of all the money you have in your life and all the money you have received in the past. Be thankful for it all. Contact three people today who have helped you financially. Really express your gratitude to them for everything they did for you, even if it only seemed small at the time.

Open my free subliminal and listen each night as you go to sleep (or in the daytime if during sleep really isn't possible) for at least 30 days.

**Share your progress with me.**

Tag me on Instagram! I'm **@francecsaamber**

Use the hashtag **#gratefulAFbook**

# DAY NINE

*Sing It Loud, Sing It Proud*

One of the most powerful ways I've found to show gratitude that takes little to no extra time or effort is to SING my gratitude!

Now, I'm no Amy Winehouse, but in the privacy of my own home, car or sometimes a gay karaoke bar I will sing my thanks to the universe as a fun, fast way to raise my vibration.

There are so many songs out there that are either purely about expressing gratitude or have the words 'thank you' in them many times.

When we practice gratitude, the more we can genuinely feel gratitude each day. The more we say and mean 'thank you' out loud the better. Feelings are a huge part of gratitude and every gratitude practice we do attempts to bring emotions and feelings into it because that's where the power lies. Music by its very nature is emotive so it's a great tool for us to use. Try and sing *'Someone Like You'* by Adele in your car whilst thinking about your regrettable ex with the devil dick and not cry. My point proven.

Now, which feels more powerful to you:

Thinking 'thank you' in your head.

Saying 'thank you' out loud for the blessings you have received.

Blasting Eternal's *'I Am Blessed'* whilst singing and crying in gratitude?

We all know the correct answer.

I have developed a ritual of playing a trio of gratitude songs each morning as I make my daughters breakfast and they go as follows:

*'Thankful'* by Beth Hart. This beautiful song has lyrics such as:

*Thank you for the laughter*
*Thank you for the chance*
*Thank you for the madness*
*Thank you for the dance*
*Thank you for forgiveness*
*And not softening the fall*
*Thank you for my love*
*Thank you for it all*
*Thank you for my life*
*I'm thankful for it all*

As I am serving up porridge and singing about thanking the universe for not softening my fall, my mind goes back to 2020, deep in the panny-D, pregnant, having lost my income, my business and my social life and 9 times out of 10 tears spring to my eyes because if that fall had been softened AT ALL, I wouldn't have been forced to just stop everything and start a podcast that changed my goddamn life. Those lyrics bring that all back to me and I feel a huge rush of gratitude that not even 100 gratitude lists could muster.

The second song is *'Another Day in Paradise'* by Phil Collins because I'm a big fan of negative visualisation. The easiest way for me to feel gratitude for something, whether it's my running water, car or mother is to imagine life without them. This song is GREAT for that. It tells the story of a lady who is homeless, cold and hungry. She asks for help but nobody does. Good old Phil asks us to:
*'Think twice, cause it's another day for you and me in paradise.'*

And he's SO right, isn't he? I can wake up in a bad mood and feel irritated that I have some errands to run today or am rushing somewhere and all I need is that song to remind me that as long as I am waking up in a bed in my house, I can afford to make my children breakfast and we're all safe - THIS IS PARADISE! Sometimes we need to be reminded and Phil Collins is just the guy.

The final song is *'I Am Blessed'* by Eternal and this song got CANED by me during my post natal depression phase. It goes a little like this:

*Though I've never seen you, somehow I know you're there*
*You're in the faces of the people I meet*
*You're as silent as the earth beneath my feet*
*So if I should complain that all I have is not enough*
*Forgive me, I've been given so much*

*And I am blessed, every time I look into my baby's eyes*
*I think of all the friends who've touched my life*
*I realise in a world where some have more and some have less*
*I am loved and I am blessed*

During my twin newborn phase I was isolated, poor, suffering from undiagnosed post natal depression and struggled to bond with my new babies. I used several songs during that time but this was definitely on the morning hit list to remind me that when I look at those babies I may be in pain, I may be sad, I may be lonely, I may be tired but I AM loved and I AM blessed.

Post natal depression is a cruel thing. It takes away all the joy and love in those early bonding days, weeks and months. Instead of revelling in my newborn bubble I would look at these unfamiliar little faces and wonder when that rush of love would come. I had felt it so strongly with my first born it had brought me to tears in a McDonalds on the side of the A1 as we drove her home from the hospital. But day after day I wondered if today would be the day that love would come. Help wasn't readily available as we were still in the grip of the pandemic. Once the babies were out nobody really asked how I was again, despite the fact I was their sole carer and nourishment. I would sit them in their bouncy chairs and play Adele's *'Make You Feel My Love'* on repeat. I would sing to them:

*I could make you happy make your dreams come true*
*Nothing that I wouldn't do*
*Go to the ends of the earth for you*
*To make you feel my love*

I would cry and wonder when those words would feel true. Spoiler alert, it worked. Time is a great healer and now I love those babies more than life itself. That song was very healing for all of us & I loved the feeling of 'doing something' to get out of the feelings I was having rather than simply waiting for it to pass.

There are so many great songs that have completely different energies.

'Gratitude' by Jason Mraz is fantastic for feeling gratitude for all the conveniences we have in life.

'Ready For Your Love' by Gorgon City makes me feel like every word is bringing my soulmate closer to me.

'Moment 4 Life' by Nikki Minaj and 'Forever' by Drake are my hype girls to get me pumped up for success.

'Money' by Cardi B & "Billionaire' by Travie McCoy & Bruno Mars are my go to songs for feeling like a wealthy woman.

There are artists who radiate gratitude and law of attraction such as Morgan St Jean whose song 'Energy (Lucky Me)' has been the soundtrack to millions of TikToks and reels about manifesting.

So today create a playlist, play it and SING IT! The vibrational shift you experience from it is like nothing else.

## Day Nine Exercise:

List three things you are grateful for as you wake up or as early in the day as you can. Make them specific to your day for bonus gratitude points!

Create a gratitude playlist and SING your gratitude!

Open my free subliminal and listen each night as you go to sleep (or in the daytime if during sleep really isn't possible) for at least 30 days.

**Share your progress with me.**

Tag me on Instagram! I'm **@francecsaamber**

Use the hashtag **#gratefulAFbook**

# DAY TEN

*So Many Brown Cars...*

Today we are going to have some fun with the universe! We are going to be testing out a fun part of your brain I bet you didn't even know you had, called the Reticular Activating System.

The reticular activating system is a neurological network in the brain responsible for filtering and prioritising sensory information. It acts as a gatekeeper, a doorman to your favourite club if you will, determining which stimuli should gain access to conscious awareness. We are subjected to an enormous amount of sensory input every second. Some estimates suggest that the brain receives around 11 million bits of information per second. However, the capacity for conscious processing is much more limited. That's where the Reticular Activating System comes in.

Essentially, the RAS helps in focusing attention on relevant cues while screening out non-essential data. This system plays a crucial role in managing the brain's limited cognitive resources, ensuring that attention is directed toward stimuli deemed important based on individual goals and priorities.

So what does that mean for us basic bitches and our

goals? Well, what we focus on, appears and grows. There are infinite possibilities open to us at all times and depending on our mood and vibration we will be aware of people, situations and opportunities that are on that vibration. This is why when you start to think about buying a Range Rover, you suddenly see Range Rovers everywhere. Your brain is focussed on Range Rovers and so your RAS picks them out in your every day reality to reinforce what you've already been thinking about.

Now think about how this can apply to your goals and it gets very exciting! If you are walking around saying life is shit, there are no opportunities or money out there then that's exactly what your RAS is going to show you. BUT if you condition yourself to seek out the positive and be sure that you are lucky, money and hot men and opportunities are possible for you then guess what - that's what you're going to see. It's SCIENCE, bitches!

Today, I want you to choose something slightly obscure to see. I almost always choose a brown car. Like, who in their right mind would choose to have a brown car? I'm not talking gold or bronze but dog poo brown.

How long has it been since you saw a brown car? Do you believe you will see a brown car today? Will you see more than one?

I LOVE to play this game with the universe and my reticular activating system because it's such a physical way to see your manifestations in front of your very eyes.

So, go about your day today and be open to seeing brown cars. Remember, just like everything you want to attract to you, they were there all along.

## Day Ten Exercise:

List three things you are grateful for as you wake up or as early in the day as you can. Make them specific to your day for bonus gratitude points!

Make a conscious decision to see brown cars today as you go about your day. If you're not going out today, simply be open to seeing them tomorrow. There's no time limit on this.

Open my free subliminal and listen each night as you go to sleep (or in the daytime if during sleep really isn't possible) for at least 30 days.

**Share your progress with me.**

Tag me on Instagram! I'm **@francecsaamber**

Use the hashtag **#gratefulAFbook**

# DAY ELEVEN

*Work It*

As we progress through this practice together I hope that your daily gratitude practices have had a real impact on both your inner and outer world. Today we are showing gratitude for our working lives, however that looks right now.

I have been in many situations throughout my working life as I'm sure you have too. I've been a student and worked in bars and clubs to make a living, I've been at college on a course I didn't resonate with, I've had temp jobs that have made me want to become a nun for the free accommodation and living expenses, I've had full time jobs with side hustles, I've been on maternity leave and had I've had part time, full blown businesses.

It doesn't matter if you live to work or work to live, there's no getting around that how we make our living has a huge impact on our lives and wellbeing, not just our finances.

Do you wake up every morning dreading your job? Are there parts of your work where you just don't give 100% and wish the time away? We all do! But today is all about showing gratitude for everything in our working life.

If you have a job, be so thankful to your employers for sorting all of your tax, sick pay and pension stuff, there's so much behind the scenes! Do you have a warm, dry workplace to work from? Is it safe? Do you have colleagues and a good work life that adds to your happiness?

If you're self employed be so thankful to all of the clients who choose to work with you, to all the suppliers who provide the products to enable you to carry out your work and the fact that you get to be your own boss.
If you're in the season of motherhood and your 'working' days are long, unpaid and tiring I FEEL YOU! But also remember that although this is the hardest job in the world, it's also the best. The days are long but the years are short (they promise) so make the most of this season.

Today I want you to create a gratitude list for everything you're thankful for in your work life. You can include your place of work, colleagues, commute, salary, tips, hours, flexibility, creativity, security and more.

Something I like to add in is gratitude for my own skills that enable me to work the way I do. I'm so thankful that my brain came up with this business, that I have the ideas I do and that I have the will power to execute them. Think of everything that contributes to your working life including your own character and skills and remember to say 'thank you, thank you, THANK YOU Universe' for each one.

As you go about your work today, in whatever capacity

that is, do your best and do everything with love and care. You would be amazed at how this simple shift makes you feel about yourself and your work. Be so thankful for everything you get to do at work from being able to listen to a podcast on your commute to having a sense of accomplishment at the end of the day.

I often talk about how much I love negative visualisation and it works especially well when thinking about our jobs or careers. Take something you complain about and imagine if you didn't have to do it. What if you didn't have a job? What if you didn't have clients? What if there was no business? You would very quickly struggle to hold on to your home, family and even your wellbeing without an income.

So whether you live to work or work to live, someone's got to pay the bills & you may as well enjoy it!

## Day Eleven Exercise:

List three things you are grateful for as you wake up or as early in the day as you can. Make them specific to your day for bonus gratitude points!

Write a gratitude list that is work-centred. Think about everything you are thankful for in your work life, whether you are employed, self employed or do unpaid work such as keeping the house or mothering. Remember to say 'thank you, thank you, THANK YOU Universe' for each one. As you go about your work day today, do all things with love, care and gratitude.

Open my free subliminal and listen each night as you go to sleep (or in the daytime if during sleep really isn't possible) for at least 30 days.

**Share your progress with me.**

Tag me on Instagram! I'm **@francecsaamber**

Use the hashtag **#gratefulAFbook**

# DAY TWELVE
*Gratitude For Food*

We can't really practice gratitude without talking about being thankful for the food we eat to keep us alive. Look, not all food keeps us alive per se, such as the third plate at the Chinese buffet or an entire tub of Angel Delight ice cream (it's a thing, try it!) But we DO owe so much thanks to the food we eat and the water we drink each day.

When was the last time you saw somebody say grace or give thanks for their food before they ate it? Unless you are a cast member of Breaking Amish or Sister Wives it's likely that it has been a very long time, if at all!

Saying grace before a meal has a rich and heartfelt history that spans cultures and time. It's like the original "thank you" note to the universe for the delightful gift of sustenance. Back in medieval times, people used to lift their goblets and give thanks to the heavens before digging into their feasts. Whether you're a knight in shining armour or a modern-day foodie, the tradition of saying grace has evolved into a delightful pause before the mealtime frenzy begins. It's a moment to express gratitude for the food before you. So, whether you're gathered around a grand feast or enjoying a humble sandwich, saying grace is like a culinary high-five to the universe, acknowledging the incredible journey from farm to fork.

Let's take a moment to savour the incredible journey our food embarks on before landing on our plates, shall we? It's like a gastronomic adventure, with our veggies and fruits going from the soil to the grocery store, surviving the perils of unpredictable weather and mischievous pests. The farmers, our unsung culinary heroes, wielding plows like knights in a veggie kingdom, deserve a standing ovation for their dedication. Then, our food eventually arrives at our local markets, ready for their grand debut. So, when we sit down to feast, let's not forget the epic quest our meals undertook to make it to our tables.

We take an endless supply of food for granted so much, yet the lack of food in the great panny-d of 2020 weren't so long ago. Do you remember when there were food shortages, supermarket shelves wiped clear of stock by panic buyers and you would give a kidney for some fresh fruit? That wasn't that long ago and yet we seem to forget so quickly.

A few years ago when pregnant with my first daughter, I recorded a video asking my mother and grandmother about their pregnancy experiences. It was kind of like a living memory box. My dear old nan talked about how there was little to no fresh fruit during the war & started crying, thinking about her own mother bringing her apples from their orchard. As someone who has HUGE fruit cravings during pregnancy, I couldn't even imagine what it was like to not be able to get hold of these basics.

Pregnancy cravings are like nothing else, I would punch someone in the gut to grab the last apple!

In the pandemic I was listed as high risk due to having an auto immune disease and being pregnant. (This sounds like I'm pregnant all the time, but I'm not!) Food delivery slots were like gold dust and I had to rely on the kindness of a local friend of a friend to go shopping for me. I remember having a huge, catering sized bag of pasta. My thoughts were, if things got really, really bad at least I could afford for me & my daughter to eat pasta with salt & olive oil.

We don't really allow ourselves to get hungry these days but if we did we would soon be crippled by the effects. The pain, the weakness, the headache the inability to think of anything else but food. When I try to feel gratitude for food I think about not being able to feed my daughters. There's nothing worse than a baby crying in hunger and I cannot imagine not being able to stop those cries. However, this is something people all over the world experience.

Today I want you to create a ritual out of at least one of your meals. Rather than just eating on the go, in your car, out of a paper bag, as you walk or watch tv I want you to prepare the table, maybe light a candle, sit and eat intentionally, say 'thank you' before you eat and think about how lucky you are to have food. Make mealtimes a shrine to your food.

I know it's hard to remember but from this day forward try to say 'thank you' to the universe, the farmers, the drivers, the packagers and the shop workers who got your food to you.

The second part of today's challenge is - I want you fully embrace the gratitude for food by donating food to your local food bank. This has been made so incredibly easy now with bins by every supermarket exit. When I do this 'gratitude for food' ritual I like to take a basket and fill it or take £20 and spend the lot. It feels GREAT to do! If you don't have the spare money right now for even one tin of beans on top of your shop then have a clear out of your cupboards and give what you can spare or won't use. A declutter AND a donation in one? Double high vibes for you my friend!

## Day Twelve Exercise:

List three things you are grateful for as you wake up or as early in the day as you can. Make them specific to your day for bonus gratitude points!

Make at least one mealtime today into a gratitude ritual. Give your mealtime and the food in it the time and space it deserves. Say 'thank you' for your food.

Donate food to a local food bank today.

Open my free subliminal and listen each night as you go to sleep (or in the daytime if during sleep really isn't possible) for at least 30 days.

(Note for tomorrow: If you wake up in the morning and instantly check your phone for social media I want you to NOT do this tomorrow. Listen to the episode tomorrow morning and you will see why.)

**Share your progress with me.**

Tag me on Instagram! I'm **@francecsaamber**

Use the hashtag **#gratefulAFbook**

# DAY THIRTEEN

*Gratitude For Time*

Today is a gratitude practice I am SO excited for!

How often do you find yourself saying you have no time? Double points if you say you have no time AND you're so tired. It's me. I'm guilty. And I'm sure you are too.

I'm going to ask you to break up. Yes, break up with what has been stealing your time, your energy, your creativity and your lust for life. YOUR PHONE!

Excessive phone and social media use is destroying our goals and dreams. It is deluding us into thinking we have no time, it's sucking our energy for it's own benefit and leaving you with the dregs. It's time to start prioritising your own life, not Mark Zuckerberg's.

Did you know we spend on average almost 4 hours a day on our phones? Half of that is on social media. We also pick up our phones to check them on average 96 times per day! Can you imagine how much time and energy that's wasting?

Now look, I love going down a Reddit rabbit hole or getting inspired on Instagram by a slow living, cottage core mama in Southern Carolina with ducklings in her kitchen sink as much as the next person. Social media can be a great tool for information, sharing our lives with loved ones and even running our businesses. However, if you find yourself saying you don't have the time or energy to start your dream business or workout or declutter your house but you DO have the time to see what your ex is doing or watch your high school friend's pyramid scheme posts then respectfully, WHAT ARE YOU DOING WITH YOUR LIFE?!? I am speaking to myself here too as I am a bugger for getting sucked into doom scrolling.

There's a great app that I discovered called Screen Zen which has been amazing for helping me to reduce my screen time. It doesn't just pop up on the screen to tell you that you've reached your limit, it actually creates space between that unconscious descision to absentmindedly open an app by asking you why you're opening it and delaying the opening by 10 seconds. Life. Changing.

Now this book isn't about breaking habits or how to have a positive relationship with your phone or social media but it IS going to ask you to do something life changing today. (Although if you DO want to break the habit for good, I can highly recommend an app called ScreenZen.)

Today I want you to not use your phone for one whole day. Obviously you can have it on and answer any calls or emails that are important and if you need to use it for work then cool, but absolutely no:

Endless scrolling of social media, in fact no social media at all.

No long, convoluted voice notes.
No online shopping.
No texting backwards and forwards.

Now I know what you're going to say. You're going to say that it's impossible, that you NEED to use your phone for social media but this is just. one. day. This experiment is not aiming to get you to throw your phone into the ocean at the end of it, but simply to show you just how much time and energy you have available to you in a day.

You will be amazed at how much you have time for. You will feel more present with the people around you, feel more connection, get things done that you've put off for ages, speed up, slow down and be right where you are.

If today is really the worst day EVER for this challenge, I will let you exchange it for tomorrow, so basically read tomorrow's challenge today and vice versa. If there are two days in a row where it really is impossible to not use your phone or social media then I would ask you to reassess your life.

Not only will you finish today feeling like you have an abundance of time and energy in your life, but you will feel so much gratitude for all of the good that our phones, social media and technology brings to our lives. The online shopping, contactless payments, being able to work remotely, looking things up in an instant and so much more.

You might want to add to your morning gratitude list today what technology has done for your life.

It's wild that we were walking around thinking that we had so little time and energy and yet it was being sucked from us by a parasite in our pocket all along.

## Day Thirteen Exercise:

List three things you are grateful for as you wake up or as early in the day as you can. Make them specific to your day for bonus gratitude points!

Put down your phone just for the day. Notice how much extra time and energy you have to do the things that matter. What will you do with it all? Answer only important calls, emails and messages. Do not touch social media!

Open my free subliminal and listen each night as you go to sleep (or in the daytime if during sleep really isn't possible) for at least 30 days.

**Share your progress with me.**

Tag me on Instagram! I'm **@francecsaamber**

Use the hashtag **#gratefulAFbook**

# DAY FOURTEEN
*Gratitude For Water*

Ok so in a previous day we showed our gratitude for food but what is it we REALLY need more than anything else? Water!

We only need to go a couple of hours without water to feel the effects on our minds and bodies. It is the number one factor for life itself.

Water, our body's backstage hero, does so much more than quenching our thirst—it's the unsung superhero of health and well-being.

Picture water as the backstage manager, coordinating a bustling show within our bodies. It keeps the temperature just right, ensuring we don't turn into human popsicles or walking saunas. Like a diligent housekeeper, water sweeps away the waste, leaving our internal abode spick and span. And let's not forget its role as the grand conductor of the nutrient orchestra, making sure every cell gets its moment in the spotlight. So, here's to water, the H2O MVP that keeps our bodies hydrated, harmonised, and happily humming along in the symphony of life.

We are primarily made up of water - a massive 65% (or slightly less when hungover!) so we would literally be a pile of dust without it.

We've all seen the footage of children in far flung countries having to walk miles to gather water, drinking dirty water that will make them sick or worse, having no water at all. We should be SO thankful every day for the water that comes out of our taps, CLEAN (Ok, ok I know we are dealing with chlorine and fluoride in our water but it's relatively clean) hot and cold straight into our homes. What a goddamn blessing!

Have you ever had no water in your house? More commonly we have experienced having no hot water, right? Remember how awful it was? What an inconvenience? This happened to me when I first moved into my little house in the country (conveniently in freezing DECEMBER!) I remember having to take 'prison showers' every day and hating every minute. A prison shower is when you fill a bucket with hot water from the kettle mixed with cold then take it to the bath or shower and use that to wash yourself.

Just the other week a plumber came to fix a toilet in my house and forgot to connect the water back to it so it didn't flush. I told everyone in the house not to use it, but of course it wasn't long until one of my children did a poo in it. Let me tell you, having a toilet that's been used and not being able to flush it for days is horrendous. It quickly smelt like a sewer in that entire bathroom. Thank goodness the plumber came back to reconnect a few days later.

So what do we have to be thankful for?

Water to flush our toilets
Water to shower or bathe
Water to drink and use in our cooking

These are just the basics and our lives would be TERRIBLE/IMPOSSIBLE without them!

Today, every time you flush the toilet, brush your teeth, shower, fill a kettle, drink a glass of water or use water in any way I want you to say and FEEL 'thank you, thank you, THANK YOU universe!'
Did you know studies have suggested that simply saying 'thank you' to our water affects its molecular structure?

Dr. Masaru Emoto was a Japanese researcher known for his unconventional studies on the potential effects of human consciousness, particularly thoughts and words, on the molecular structure of water. His work gained popularity through his book, "The Hidden Messages in Water," published in 2004.

Dr. Emoto conducted experiments where he exposed water to various conditions, including different words and then observed the formation of water crystals using microscopic photography. His claim was that positive and negative words, emotions, or music could influence the molecular structure of water.

In his experiments, Dr. Emoto suggested that positive words, thoughts, and emotions resulted in the formation of symmetrical and aesthetically pleasing water crystals, while negative influences led to distorted or incomplete crystal structures. He believed that since the human body is largely composed of water, these findings had implications for human health and well-being.

While Dr. Emoto's work garnered attention, it's essential to note that his methods and conclusions faced criticism within the scientific community. Traditional scientific research typically requires rigorous experimental design, reproducibility, and peer-reviewed publication. Some critics argued that Dr. Emoto's studies lacked these elements and were more anecdotal than scientifically robust.

Despite the controversy, Dr. Emoto's work has sparked interest and discussions about the potential interplay between human consciousness and the environment.

Isn't that wild? You can try a number of Dr Emoto's water experiments with potatoes or rice where it is easier to see the results.

Anyway, back to our gratitude for water. Personally, I pour my water for each day into a large, ceramic jug and leave it to stand, pouring from that throughout the day as I need it. As I pour the water into it I think about how thankful I am for clean water and I find that easier to be so thankful for the entire jug rather than every time I have to turn that tap on as I know I'll forget.

Today I want you to not only be thankful for the water you use throughout the day but also to turn your shower or bath into a ceremonial, ritualistic, gratitude-filled experience.

Turning your shower or bath into a ceremonial and mindful experience can be a wonderful way to promote relaxation, self-care, and mindfulness. Here are some suggestions to help you create a more ceremonial atmosphere:

**Set the Mood**:

Dim the lights or use candles to create a soothing ambiance.

Consider using essential oils or scented candles to enhance the sensory experience.

**Choose Thoughtful Products**:

Select bath products or shower gels with calming scents or ingredients that you enjoy.

Opt for natural and nourishing products to enhance the sensory experience.

**Create Rituals:**

Develop a set routine or series of actions that mark the beginning and end of your shower or bath.

This could include lighting a specific candle, using a particular scrub, or incorporating a short meditation.

**Mindful Cleansing:**

Instead of rushing through your shower, take the time to be present with each step.

Pay attention to the sensation of the water, the scent of

the products, and the feeling of self-care.

**Use Visualisation:**

Close your eyes and visualise the water cleansing not just your body but also your mind and spirit.

Imagine stress and tension washing away with each drop.

**Incorporate Music or Sounds:**

Play calming music, nature sounds or even your favourite podcast in the background to enhance the experience.

Consider creating a playlist specifically for your ceremonial showers or baths.

**Express Gratitude:**

Take a moment to express gratitude for the water, the products you're using, and the time you've set aside for self-care.

**Intention Setting:**

Before stepping into the shower or bath, set a positive intention for the experience.

Reflect on what you want to release or invite into your life.

**Post-Shower Ritual:**

Extend the ceremonial experience by using a luxurious lotion or oil after your shower.

Take a moment to appreciate the refreshed and relaxed state you're in.

I hope that you really enjoy today's exercise and tailor it to your needs. If it's the height of summer as you're reading this and you have a busy day, it could be as simple as putting some music on as you shower and taking a few extra moments to really feel the gratitude. If it's the depths of winter and you have a little more time then a slow, nourishing baths sounds perfect. So long as you practice gratitude, that's all that matters.

## Day Fourteen Exercise:

List three things you are grateful for as you wake up or as early in the day as you can. Make them specific to your day for bonus gratitude points!

Today is all about gratitude for water. Say 'thank you' each time you use water today, consider blessing your water with gratitude and take a mindful bath or shower.

Open my free subliminal and listen each night as you go to sleep (or in the daytime if during sleep really isn't possible) for at least 30 days.

**Share your progress with me.**

Tag me on Instagram! I'm **@francecsaamber**

Use the hashtag **#gratefulAFbook**

# DAY FIFTEEN

*I Get To...*

Today we are focussing on a simple mindset shift from 'I have to' to 'I get to'.

It's so simple but it really does show you that you have so much to be thankful for in your every day life.

I know that life can be busy, it can be stressful and it can be hard. It can sometimes feel like you have too many plates spinning and that you won't get everything done. I've been there too. I have days where I have to get three children up and out by 8:30am, deal with lots of life admin, maybe the plumber is coming at lunchtime to fix the washing machine, get all my work done, make my hair appointment, go food shopping, make the dinner, do a laborious nit treatment (AGAIN) on everyone and make sure everyone gets to bed on time otherwise they turn into Gremlins. Sounds like a busy and stressful day right? But simply changing the 'I have to' into 'I get to' is a powerful mindset shift.

I GET to get my three children up and out at 8:30am because I live in a country where we have incredible education and childcare. I get to wake up three healthy children - how lucky am I? Would I prefer not to have them? Would I prefer they didn't live with me? Of course not! Thank you universe.

I GET to deal with life admin today. Each piece of admin such as paying an electricity bill means I get to receive the benefits of that service. How lucky am I? Thank you universe.

I GET to have a working washing machine today which means I can have freshly laundered clothes without leaving my house, thank you universe.

I GET to work today on my dream career - how lucky am I? This is going to give me purpose, passion and pay me. I can use that money to live in my home, eat, go out and so much more.

I GET to have my hair done today! What a blessing! Ok, so it's the patriarchy that have decided that my grey hair is unacceptable and must be covered so respectfully, fuck them! But still, I know I am helping a local hair stylist by paying her and I will feel fabulous after, thank you universe.

I GET to go food shopping and make dinner - what a miracle! I have local food shops which are fully stocked with everything I need and I have a kitchen to cook the food in for me and my family. Thank you universe.

(I recently went several months with no kitchen and it was hellish. I basically did a tour of the local supermarket cafes on repeat and became such a regular in The Harvester that they knew our names and orders. It started out as fun but became very expensive and I genuinely worried we were going to get scurvy from the lack of vegetables. I will never take a kitchen for granted again!)

I GET to do a head lice treatment on all my children again, what a joy! Imagine if these treatments didn't exist or we didn't have such things as head lice combs? Eurgh. I can turn it into a fun, bonding experience and use the time to really talk and sing songs and whatever else. Some people don't have access to head lice treatment and that must be terrible. Thank you universe.

I GET to put my children to bed tonight in a warm, safe home. How lucky am I? There are mothers around the world that would give anything to be able to do the same. As I do it I will think of the mothers who are experiencing famine, genocide, war, domestic abuse, homelessness and more. I will be so thankful that I get to do this, thank you universe.

As you can see, my busy day of 'have to's' suddenly gets turned into its very own gratitude list. We can become immune to seeing the blessings all around us and turning our have to's into get to's is a great way to become aware once more.

Today I want you to write out your 'to-do's' for the day and turn your tasks into blessings. As you complete each one really think about why it's such a blessing you get to do this.

Sometimes we will have days that are very tough and we won't be able to see a blessing in our tasks but they are

ALWAYS there.

Going to the most extreme, if today you are having to bury a loved one, we can be thankful that we got to know and love them, that we get to say goodbye. There are so many people that have children or loved ones go missing and never get that closure.

We can always turn our 'ugh, I have to....' Into 'wow, I get to' at any point and I can't wait for you to see how this changes your world.

## Day Fifteen Exercise:

List three things you are grateful for as you wake up or as early in the day as you can. Make them specific to your day for bonus gratitude points!

Today turn your to do list into a gratitude list by reframing each task from 'I have to' to 'I get to'.

Open my free subliminal and listen each night as you go to sleep (or in the daytime if during sleep really isn't possible) for at least 30 days.

**Share your progress with me.**

Tag me on Instagram! I'm **@francecsaamber**

Use the hashtag **#gratefulAFbook**

# DAY SIXTEEN

*Gratitude for Transport*

Today I want you to think about how you get around. Transport is such a vital part of life and we would be lost without it.

There's a great documentary called 'Crip Camp' that I would love you to watch.

"Crip Camp" is an inspiring documentary that takes us back to the 1970s, where a group of teenagers with disabilities discovered a summer camp in upstate New York that became a transformative experience. This wasn't just any camp—it was a place where friendships blossomed, love bloomed, and a fierce sense of empowerment ignited. From the lively campfire discussions to the unstoppable spirit of activism that emerged, the film captures the essence of Camp Jened, a special haven where campers embraced their quirks and differences. As these campers grew up, their journey extended beyond the campgrounds, evolving into a powerful movement for disability rights. "Crip Camp" is a celebration of resilience, friendship, and the belief that everyone deserves a seat at the table—and on the bus. It's a documentary that will have you cheering, laughing, and maybe shedding a tear or two as you witness the extraordinary impact of a summer that changed lives and helped change the world.

This documentary will have you thinking about how lucky we are to be able to access the public transport, restaurants and shops we do without issue. And if you're disabled it will give you enormous gratitude to the people who fought for accessibility rights.

Whatever mode of transport you use day to day doesn't matter. You might walk to school, get the bus, train or tram to work or drive to the shops - imagine your life without any of these modes of transport. For some of us it might be a lot harder and lengthier to get things done. For others it would be impossible.

We only need to experience one blip in the chain to feel the full force of having no transport. It could be a crash that closes the road, a train drivers strike that brings the rails to a standstill or having your car break down at the side of the road on a cold, rainy night.

I want you to show so much gratitude today for your journeys, wherever they take you. For me this looks like:

Today I'm driving my car to visit my family. I'm so thankful for all the people who planned and built the roads. It's icy today so I'm thankful for the local council who gritted the roads early this morning, made warning signs and light the streets for us to see. I'm so thankful for my car which has been so reliable and gets me from A to B. I'm so thankful to the people who keep it in good repair and for the fuel that is readily available for me to buy. Thank you universe.

Now, I do love a physical action to go with my gratitude as I feel it super charges it and we can do this in so many ways.
If you ride a bike or walk to get around you can show so much gratitude for your body for getting you could show gratitude to your body by booking in a leg or foot massage or giving yourself a foot spa.

If you regularly catch the bus you could say to the driver 'I'm so glad you're here today - you've made my life so much easier'.

If you get the train you could DM the provider saying 'thank you for always providing a great service - getting to work without you would be so hard.'

If you use your car you could give it a treat and show it some gratitude. Clear out all the clutter, take it to a car wash if you have time, hang some protection crystals in there (google: Crystal car charms) and tell your car 'thank you!'

I hope this practice really highlights all the work that goes into us getting around safely, quickly and easily that we so often take for granted.

## Day Sixteen Exercise:

List three things you are grateful for as you wake up or as early in the day as you can. Make them specific to your day for bonus gratitude points!

Today, turn your gratitude to how you get around. Which modes of transport are you so thankful for and how can you show them?

Open my free subliminal and listen each night as you go to sleep (or in the daytime if during sleep really isn't possible) for at least 30 days.

**Share your progress with me.**

Tag me on Instagram! I'm **@francecsaamber**

Use the hashtag **#gratefulAFbook**

# DAY SEVENTEEN

*Gratitude for Bills & Services*

We all get bills, we all have stuff we pay for and sometimes we resent having to pay out for things. I get it. It's fun to go shopping for a new bag or outfit but is it sexy paying your gas, electric or childcare bill? Nah.

I want us to turn that around today and be so thankful for all the bills and services we pay for that help us to live our best goddamn lives.

In the past, old-fashioned gratitude practices would have you pay paper bills and write thank you on them but we're in 2024 baby (currently!) and that's not the way we move anymore. You most likely pay your recurring bills via an automatic subscription so you don't even have to physically do anything to pay that bill. It's great to automate these things so it takes up less of our time & energy but it also means we can take these services for granted.

I want you to think about all of the services and subscriptions you pay for (and maybe some you don't) and find a few that really have changed your life for the better.

Think about the help around the home we get. Do you

get food shopping delivered, a cleaner, do you buy meal kits or prepared meals that make life easier? Maybe it's the bin men who take your rubbish away reliably each week.

How about at work? Do you use any services to run your business or in your job? For me, I would really struggle to get the word out about my podcast without social media, I wouldn't be able to release it at all without my hosting platform and I wouldn't be able to earn money without my subscription podcast. I also pay individual people who help me in so many aspects of running the show.

What about entertainment? Do you have a Netflix subscription? Do you have certain creators that provide you with LOLs for free or give you amazing advice? Maybe you have certain apps that you use religiously (for me it's the free app Stardust that allows me to track my period AND the moon - what a witch!)

Today I want you to think of 3 to 5 companies, services or people that you pay (or some might be free - even more gratitude!) thank them and even shout them out on social media if applicable.

For me, mine would be:

When the supermarket food delivery comes I will say to the driver: "I was just thinking how thankful I am that you provide this service. Thank you so much."

I will DM the podcast provider Acast and thank them for making advertising revenue on podcasts so easy and effortless. It took me nearly three years to figure out how I can get podcast sponsorship effortlessly and I'm so thankful for that passive income.

I will shoutout the free Stardust app on social media to help boost their subscribers as it's such a fantastic app for tracking tour period, hormones and the moon.

I will take a little gift into my children's nursery for the women that take care of them and teach them whilst I'm working to show my thanks for all they do.

If I get good service somewhere, particularly in a big chain I will DM the company giving the name and location of the worker and say they went above and beyond to help me (you can always do this retrospectively too) It's likely the company will reward that person.

I will comment on my favourite online creator's latest post thanking them for all the entertainment/ knowlege/information they provide for free.

So as you can see, you can mix up your gratitude across all different kinds of services both paid and unpaid. But sharing that gratitude will spread joy and smiles across the globe to wherever they land.

## Day Seventeen Exercise:

List three things you are grateful for as you wake up or as early in the day as you can. Make them specific to your day for bonus gratitude points!

Make a list of services you pay for (and some you don't) and thank them for what they bring to your life. They could be huge corporations such as Netflix or as specific as saying 'thank you, you really helped me today' to someone who serves you in a store. Aim to say a heartfelt 'thank you' and the reason why to 3-5 services today, however you feel comfortable doing so.

Open my free subliminal and listen each night as you go to sleep (or in the daytime if during sleep really isn't possible) for at least 30 days.

**Share your progress with me.**

Tag me on Instagram! I'm **@francecsaamber**

Use the hashtag **#gratefulAFbook**

# DAY EIGHTEEN

*Romanticise Your Life*

Romanticising your life is a concept I came across only relatively recently and let me tell you - it's changed my goddamn life!

It's about taking every day moments, normal, ordinary things - even the mundane and turning them into joyful, mindful rituals. Now sometimes this can be seen externally. As I write this right now I am at a service station on the A1. I often come here to collect my daughters from their time with their dad. I find it a bit of a stressful place, full of people and me full of anxiety.

Usually I would sit in the same spot outside McDonald's, get some unhealthy fast food, scroll my phone mindlessly and await their arrival. Today I decided to turn up an hour early and discovered a beautiful (ok, maybe not beautiful, I mean this is a service station) glass-fronted mezzanine level that overlooks the whole place. It's much quieter up here. I ordered some healthy, Mexican food and took a table next to a large, twinkly Christmas tree and settled in to write this book.

You can see how just by making a few subtle differences to my environment, I've now created an enjoyable, cosy experience for myself during something I otherwise would endure rather than enjoy. You can do this in so many ways.

Do you normally hate your drive to work? Could you make it more enjoyable by getting the temperature just right before you set off so you don't drive in your coat, you can be comfortable instead? You could pre download your favourite podcast to enjoy along the way and maybe take a flask of hot chocolate with you? Can you tell I am writing this in the dead of winter?

In the evening instead of flopping onto the sofa, turning the tv on and then scrolling on your phone simultaneously, could you instead light some candles and lamps, get a cosy blanket, make yourself a snack or hot drink and consciously choose to turn your phone off and either watch a movie or read a book? Give yourself the gift of hygge!

There are countless ways we can subtly change the environment or how we do things that will romanticise our lives that you can see externally like this, but other times the change is more inside our minds. Don't let this fool you into thinking it's not just as powerful.

Sometimes the narrative inside our heads is all we need to romanticise our lives. We can picture our every day life as a plot in a rom com or an inspirational documentary. It turns the mundane into the exciting.

I did this just recently on a trip to London. I was there all weekend to see my friends and was in a time and space were I was VERY open to the possibility of love and romance. I was child-free, had a day of fun planned with different friends, had done my hair and make up, dressed nicely and it was just before Christmas - what a time to be alive!

Now in the past I had often done this exact same ritual - made fun plans with friends, dressed nicely, worn makeup and thought 'ooh, I wonder who I will meet today?' And guess who I met each time? NOBODY! This time was different. I had recently learnt about romanticising your life and so I was walking around that day as if I were in the new Richard Curtis Christmas rom com blockbuster. Everything was a story, an opportunity. Very shortly after, I made long, lingering eye contact with a hot man at a restaurant we were visiting and rather than just letting it pass me by I kinda kept it going during our time there. I fully embraced the rom com storyline that was now my life and long story short - we exchanged numbers and a new connection was made. At the time of writing this I've only 'known' him for a day, we're exchanging voice notes and planning to meet up next time I'm there but you know what, it kinda doesn't matter what the outcome is. What matters is that we had that 'moment', my friends and I very much enjoyed the chase and the flirt and it was exciting!

You can make so many more moments in your life magical and exciting if you just let them be. You can turn the ordinary into the extraordinary. It's time to be the lead in the story of your life, to up your main character energy and LIVE the fairytale. That's exactly what we are going to do today.

Whatever you have planned or you find yourself doing today - make it magical.

## Day Eighteen Exercise:

List three things you are grateful for as you wake up or as early in the day as you can. Make them specific to your day for bonus gratitude points!

Make it your mission to romanticise your life today in any way you can. Make the ordinary things extraordinary by filling them full of care, love and joy. Put in that little extra effort and see how you feel.

Remember you can even just do this internally, by playing out your day as if you were in your favourite rom com or inspirational documentary.

Open my free subliminal and listen each night as you go to sleep (or in the daytime if during sleep really isn't possible) for at least 30 days.

**Share your progress with me.**

Tag me on Instagram! I'm **@francecsaamber**

Use the hashtag **#gratefulAFbook**

# DAY NINETEEN

*Create a High Vibe*

Today we are going to focus purely on raising our vibration by doing something we love and that puts us in a high vibration. Now, before you pull out your phone and scroll, binge eat everything in your fridge or call that toxic dick appointment you've done so well to avoid - there's a BIG difference between what you WANT to do and what will make you happy/raise your vibration.

Our brains will always choose the path of least resistance and what will bring us a 'high' whether that's sugar, alcohol, a dopamine hit of getting likes on social media or getting a text back from aforementioned toxic dick appointment. But we're talking about a REAL high here, a high vibration.

Think about what activities make you really happy. They're activities that maybe take a little extra time or effort than the ones I mentioned above but when you've done them, you feel so much better for it.

Engaging in activities you love is like pressing the "joy" button in the grand orchestra of life. It's the magical elixir that elevates your spirit, turning ordinary moments into dazzling good vibes. Whether you're dancing like no one's watching, embracing your inner filmmaker, or just cozying up with a favourite book, these moments of passion and delight act as the ultimate mood boosters. Picture it as a cosmic handshake with the universe, exchanging high-fives of positivity and radiance. So dive into the activities that make your heart do the happy dance – you'll be cranking up your vibrational frequency and turning your everyday existence into a cosmic carnival of bliss. After all, who knew that a little self-love and joyous indulgence could be the secret sauce for a positively vibrating life? Cheers to raising the vibes, one joyful moment at a time!

Take out your journal or a notepad and write a list of activities that leave you feeling happy, high vibe and with more energy than before. For me it's the following:

Reading a book uninterrupted
Watching an entire crime documentary without looking at my phone
Photography - especially when it's of my children
Taking a hot bath and listening to my favourite podcast
Being creative
Hygge
Spending time with family and friends
Attending a women's circle
Visiting new places

Today I want you to commit to doing just one activity that will raise your vibration. This may fall on a busy day and so for me it might be that I only have time to have a bath whilst listening to a podcast. But if I had a little more time I would dress my daughters up in the cutest outfits, head outside to a leafy lane or the stream in our village and take some amazing pictures.

As we lead increasingly busy lives we can feel guilty taking time out to do something just for the fun of it. I don't know about you but I often feel like I have to be 'productive' - but don't fall into that never-ending trap. Number one, we should never be too busy for fun but number two, partaking in activities which make you feel great and raise your vibration is one of the best ways to align with goals which you want to manifest.

When we talk about being on the same vibration as our desires it can feel impossible. Maybe you want to double your income, meet the love of your life or write a bestselling book. But when you look at the base reason for wanting to achieve any of those goals, the reason is almost always to feel happy. You want to double your income because you think the extra money and freedom will bring you happiness. You want to meet the love of your life because you believe he or she will make you happy. You want to write a bestselling book because the process, achievement and recognition of that will make you happy. These goals may very well bring you happiness but you can also experience it right here, right now. The more you get on the vibrational frequency of happiness now, the more will be attracted to you in the future.

If you're compiling a list of your high vibe activities for this book, you may as well keep that list handy and refer back to it whenever you need a vibrational shift.

## Day Nineteen Exercise:

List three things you are grateful for as you wake up or as early in the day as you can. Make them specific to your day for bonus gratitude points!

Make a list of activities that raise your vibration. Really think about what you love to do and that makes you feel more excited for life. Pick one activity today to raise your vibration and give it the time, energy and space it deserves.

Open my free subliminal and listen each night as you go to sleep (or in the daytime if during sleep really isn't possible) for at least 30 days.

**Share your progress with me.**

Tag me on Instagram! I'm **@francecsaamber**

Use the hashtag **#gratefulAFbook**

# DAY TWENTY

*Gratitude For The Shit*

Today might be a tough day for you to do, but I promise it will transform the way you view negative people, circumstances and events in your life. As we approach the end of this gratitude process I think you're ready for it.

We all want a beautiful life full of amazing relationships, great opportunities, money, freedom, health, excitement and more. The reality is for most people they have a situation or a person that blights their happiness.

Today I want you to think of the worst situation or person in your life right now. It is most likely that one will pop into your head right away. We are going to transform this situation using the power of gratitude.

In case you are still unclear on what to choose I will give you some examples.

A shitty ex who continues to try and control your life long after a breakup
A co worker who seems to be out to ruin your career
An illness or condition which affects your enjoyment of life
A job which makes you sad

Housing that isn't suitable for your needs
A family member who constantly talks down to you

I now want you to write a gratitude list all about that person or situation. I know that you might recoil at the very thought of that, insisting that there isn't a single thing you be grateful for about this person or situation but I promise you there is.

I used to have an ex that would try to make my life hell and I couldn't get rid of him. Every time he broke up with somebody new it would be me that felt the full wrath of it. Whenever the messages and demands got too much and I felt myself becoming overwhelmed with fear, anger and sadness I would surprise my family and friends by suddenly declaring 'I need to write a gratitude list about him!'

I'm excited to inform you, it works every single time for me.

Two things to remember if your chosen subject today is a person (even if you choose an event or situation, its likely to be attributed somewhat to human beings).

Number one is that most people are just doing the best with the information and knowledge they have. Not everyone has had the idea to work on themselves or the opportunity, so we must allow people to be as evolved emotionally as they are. We can't expect everyone to think like us. Number two when dealing with difficult people is to look at everything though a lens of love. When it seems like people are doing their best to destroy us we only need to add the filter of 'love' and we can see things differently.

Navigating life's endless parade of characters and situations with a lens of love is like putting on heart-shaped sunglasses – suddenly, everything looks a bit brighter and more colourful. When faced with challenging people or situations, choosing to see them through the filter of love becomes an act of cosmic jujitsu. Instead of engaging in a tug-of-war with negativity, you're performing a love-filled pirouette around it. It's like sending good vibes into the universe and inviting them to join your positivity party. So, when confronted with an unpleasant person or a tough situation, channel your inner Cupid, shoot some love arrows, and watch how the whole vibe transforms into compassion and understanding.

So take out your journal or notebook and write out a list of everything you are thankful for in that person. Dig deep, I know you can find some gems because I do every single time no matter how miserable they are trying to make my life.

As you finish this exercise think about the situation or the person again in your mind but with this new lens of love and gratitude and say 'thank you universe for resolving this person/situation with me, I am READY to see the solution'. Spoiler alert, sometimes the solution isn't that the person gets hit by a bus but is simply that you now feel differently about it in your own mind.

## Day Twenty Exercise:

List three things you are grateful for as you wake up or as early in the day as you can. Make them specific to your day for bonus gratitude points!

Make a gratitude list about one negative person or situation which is the bane of your life. Reframe it in your mind and be open to co-create with the universe for the perfect solution.

Open my free subliminal and listen each night as you go to sleep (or in the daytime if during sleep really isn't possible) for at least 30 days.

**Share your progress with me.**

Tag me on Instagram! I'm **@francecsaamber**

Use the hashtag **#gratefulAFbook**

# DAY TWENTY ONE

*Lucky Girl Syndrome*

We're almost at the end of our journey! I'm so happy to diagnose you with 'Lucky Girl Syndrome'.

Lucky Girl Syndrome is a term that captures the phenomenon where someone seems to effortlessly attract good fortune or positive outcomes in various aspects of their life. It's like they have a four-leaf clover permanently tucked into their Spanx, sprinkling luck wherever they go. Whether it's career opportunities falling into place, serendipitous encounters, or winning those Insta competitions for spa days or free gifts without breaking a sweat, individuals with Lucky Girl Syndrome appear to have a charmed existence.

Of course, by now you should know that we are all creating our own 'luck'. This phenomenon is often observed in those who radiate positive energy, maintain an optimistic outlook, and approach challenges with resilience and enthusiasm. It's not about luck raining down from the heavens but more about cultivating a mindset that magnetises positive experiences.

While using the term 'Lucky Girl Syndrome' might sound like a playful notion, it highlights the power of mindset and attitude in shaping our experiences.

Embracing positivity, being open to opportunities, and approaching life with gratitude can indeed create an atmosphere where luck seems to be a constant companion.

Today we are going to wake up and set the intention: 'I am a lucky girl. I have lucky girl syndrome and I am going to have an amazing day.'

Read the following affirmations to yourself, out loud if you can:

I am a lucky girl

I have lucky girl syndrome

Fortune follows me effortlessly, like a trail of stardust

Today is going to be an incredible day

Luck is my loyal companion, and good things happen to me every day

I attract positivity and opportunities like a magnet

Every challenge is an opportunity for luck to shine in my favour

My life is a series of fortunate events, and the best is yet to come

I am a lucky charm, and luck radiates from me in all direction

Serendipity is my middle name; I attract unexpected joys

My positive energy creates a lucky aura around me

Opportunities unfold effortlessly, and luck paves my path

I am a magnet for miracles, big and small

I am open to miracles happening today

Every setback is a setup for a lucky comeback

Luck is my co-pilot, steering me toward success and happiness

I am a lucky charm, and positivity is my superpower

The universe conspires in my favour always

With each breath, I inhale luck and exhale gratitude

I am a lucky girl, and my life is a tapestry woven with threads of good fortune

As you go about your day today be open to being the luckiest person in the room, good things happening and the universe conspiring in your favour.

## Day Twenty One Exercise:

List three things you are grateful for as you wake up or as early in the day as you can. Make them specific to your day for bonus gratitude points!

Read aloud your 'lucky girl syndrome' affirmations and set the intention that today is going to be a lucky day.

Open my free subliminal and listen each night as you go to sleep (or in the daytime if during sleep really isn't possible) for at least 30 days.

**Share your progress with me.**

Tag me on Instagram! I'm **@francecsaamber**

Use the hashtag **#gratefulAFbook**

# DAY TWENTY TWO

*The Final Day*

Here we are, we've reached the final day! If you have got this far then well done. It's not easy to stick to a new habit for 22 days, but I hope you can see the difference that daily gratitude has made to your life.

Today I want you to think about something you would really like to manifest. Not your top ten biggest hits or a goal for each area of your life - just one thing.

Don't overthink it or worry about it too much, just choose something that excites you if it manifested. I sometimes worry about not choosing the 'right' one but the good news is, as your gratitude muscle builds and grows you will find it easier and easier to manifest time after time so you can slowly plough through your list of goals and desires. Ensure that your goal is specific as possible.

Write your goal or desire out in the following format:

I am so thankful I have manifested (insert desire here) into my life because (insert how it will improve your life or how it will make you feel here) thank you, thank you, THANK YOU universe!

Now we are going to infuse your life with that goal, desire or intention.

Stick that piece of paper somewhere you will see it every day. You could put it on your fridge or your mirror.

Make it the screensaver of your phone and laptop so that you see it 100+ times a day (unless you took day 13 very seriously!)

Create a vision board dedicated solely to this goal or desire.

Set a reminder on your phone to pop up once a day at a time to suit you with that exact goal written out that exact way.

Write out a list of affirmations that support that goal and repeat them daily. If you're a time-poor or lazy bitch like me, you could simply record yourself saying them into a voice note and listen to that each day whilst you get ready or are doing tasks around the house.

Visualise your goal regularly. There's no need to set aside any specific time for this, you can simply do this whilst you're walking, working out, commuting, cleaning or having a shower. I find it most powerful to EMBODY the feeling of having it NOW. You can do this by playing 'pretend' - act as if your desire is here right now.

Create a vacuum - clear out where necessary because the universe loves a goddamn vacuum. Want to attract a new man? Clear out half your wardrobe to make space for him. Want to attract new friendships into your life?

Clear out your schedule to make time for them and cut the dead wood of friendships that have long expired. Want to manifest a dream house? Hire a skip and declutter as if you are moving tomorrow.

Decluttering and creating a vacuum is very powerful because not only are you taking a physical action (the universe LOVES a physical action) but you are creating space for what you want AND you are moving energy. It's a win-win-win.

Finally take a positive, impactful action towards it. Just take action and the universe will join you to co create the life of your dreams.

Is The Party Over?

The party has only just begun my friend. Gratitude is just the first step in the journey of manifesting, the law of attraction and self development, albeit a very powerful one. I am over 15 years into my law of attraction journey and I STILL forget that sometimes the only magic needed is gratitude.

Some of these exercises will have resonated with you more than others and that's fine. Take the ones you love and continue to apply them into your life.

Some people get disappointed when they can't manifest right away, but developing the skill of manifestation, gratitude and a positive mindset is the same as any other skill you need to learn. You can't just expect to get it 100% straight away, much like you wouldn't step off the plane in Malaga for your first time in Spain and expect to be able to speak Spanish fluently.

A positive mindset is not only a skill but a muscle too - one that needs working out regularly. Would you go to the gym for one workout then expect to have a six pack? Hardly, and the same is true here. Gratitude and a positive mindset is not something you do once but something you practice daily in your life.

This book may be over but there are so many other ways we can continue the journey together. I host a self development book club with a gorgeous, high vibe community of book club bitches that I would love you to be a part of. Each month we choose a new book that will improve our lives and although it's mostly straight up, hard core law of attraction we have also read about Feng shui and how your home can become your living vision board, how to dress for the life you want, how decluttering makes space for what you desire in your life, how to overcome money blocks to become a wealthy woman and SO much more.

I also host a weekly podcast called 'Law of Attraction Changed My Life' and offer guided meditations, subliminals and so much more all over on my website francescaamber.com

I truly hope you have enjoyed this book and that gratitude becomes a natural part of your life. There will be times I guarantee you will forget all about this and slide back into a negative space, letting spiralling thoughts consume you, but this book & gratitude will always welcome you back with open arms, ready to help you achieve all you desire in this lifetime.

## The Beginning.

# ABOUT THE AUTHOR

**Francesca Amber**

Francesca Amber is SINGLE and one of the UK's most successful podcasters, sharing her thoughts on the law of attraction with thousands of listeners each week.
She lives with her three daughters and reluctantly a hamster until it dies in Lincolnshire and Islington, London.

Find her on Instragram @francescaamber
francescaamber.com

Printed in Great Britain
by Amazon

35920768R00066